GW00360239

MEDITATION
AND THE
FULNESS OF LIFE

by

JIM WILSON

JAMES CLARKE & CO. LTD.
7 All Saints Passage
Cambridge

First Published 1974

Reprinted 1979

ISBN 0 227 67810 9

David Green (Printers) Ltd, Kettering, Northamptonshire

FOREWORD

In a life of 91 years, Fr. Jim wrote fully about Parish life and Prayer. In this volume his later thoughts on Meditation are summarised. It is the work of several hands. It was prepared by Miss Sheila Shennan, a member of one of Fr. Jim's Meditation groups at Harpenden, from tape-recordings made during the last few years. She has arranged them to follow as closely as possible the method he used, and she wishes to thank Miss Evelyn Norman for the use of the tape-recordings and Miss Cora Rodda for help throughout the preparation of the manuscript. The Rev. Dr. Arthur Jones has edited and prepared the book for publication, and a contribution from a Thanksgiving Fund in Fr. Jim's memory is being made towards its production.

The names of individuals mentioned in the talks have been altered to preserve anonymity.

CONTENTS

I The method

The purpose of meditation is to help us to become more deeply aware of the presence of God and of the activity of His life. His spirit fills both heaven and earth; it is in us, in every single human being in the world. There is nowhere in the whole of creation where He is not. "Lo, I am with you, always" (Matt. 28. 20).

One of the purposes of a Prayer Group is to help us to get a sense of our unity with one another and of our unity with the whole creation. Then in the stillness we come to know the reality of God's presence, of what He is really like, and of what His purpose is, not only for ourselves, but for all the world. The value of our meditation is not to be judged by whether we like it particularly; it has nothing to do with feelings.

We begin by trying to relax and be still. We are so seldom actually still and quiet, but it is perfectly possible. It is best to sit in an upright chair with both feet flat on the floor, with a straight back and your head up, hands resting on your lap, and with your eyes closed. Let go of any stiffness and tension, relaxing your feet and legs, your arms and then your hands. Your hands are very sensitive instruments of the body and it is very important for them to be relaxed—you will probably find they are most comfortable lying one over the other, palms up.

Now relax your stomach muscles. This is important because from here, in your middle are controlled so many of the glands which affect the well-being of the whole body. Then your neck and face, particularly your jaw. You will be surprised how much tension there is in your face. We tend, especially if we are over-tired or anxious, to hold our teeth tight together and to screw up our cheeks and forehead. Lastly your eyes—even your eyes hold a tremendous amount of tension. It also helps to take one or two deep breaths, relaxing as you breathe out.   At first you may have to practise this a number of times, but you will soon find that you can relax quite quickly.

Once you are relaxed in body, you try to get really still and quiet in mind.   The mind is very restless; it flits about from one thing to another all day long and at first it is very difficult to keep it quiet.   People vary a great deal in how long it takes them to learn to do this.

We then give the conscious mind a phrase or short sentence to hold in the silence, not something to think about, just to hold, so that the truth of the words can sink deeply.

So let us be still for just a few moments, realising God's presence and saying slowly, over and over in our minds the words

INFINITE PEACE WITHIN

SILENCE

Thanksgiving: Father, we thank Thee that Thy peace is with us and in us.

We always end our meditation with thanksgiving.

To begin with, we keep quiet for a very short time, but as we persevere with the training of our minds we find we are able to take a longer period for meditation.   It may seem to be very difficult to find time for meditation, but we do find time for what we think important—we find time to wash and do our hair, for instance.   It is very important to meditate every day, preferably first thing in the morning, then later as well if possible.   Most people use the same sentence for a week, then change it.   At a group meeting we usually take three different meditations, linked by a central thought.

Now let us take a slightly longer meditation.

INFINITE PEACE WITHIN I WOULD LEARN OF THEE

SILENCE

Thanksgiving: Thanks be to God. "They that wait upon the Lord shall renew their strength." Teach us, dear Lord, how to wait on Thee in this simple way.

The creative life which pervades all life—the plants, the animals and man—is the spirit of God (the Good One). We say that God is good, but what do we mean by "good"? We mean that He is love, love which is not selfish or possessive but cares for others and goes out in goodwill. We mean that He is joy, wisdom, beauty, truth. He is light, justice, peace and holiness (wholeness).

Because God *is* love, *is* peace, *is* joy, and because God's life is already within us, these qualities are already within us. This means that we have no need to ask Him for them. We have no need to beg and beseech Him, as if He were a sort of wonder worker in the sky who would do things if we badgered Him enough. What we are seeking in silent meditation is to draw out the goodness of God already within us into expression, so that we may be able to express His spirit in our lives. His spirit is all that we need; it is completely adequate to all our needs.

In our final meditation we will hold in our minds again the thought of God's peace within us.

BE STILL AND KNOW MY PEACE WITHIN

SILENCE

Thanksgiving: Praise God in His holiness, praise Him in all the world. We praise and worship Thee, dear Lord, and give Thee thanks for our fellowship together.

So we go forth in peace.

II Conscious, sub-conscious and unconscious

Let us try to get quiet, realising our unity with each other and with the whole of God's creation. We relax the body, and then try to relax the mind. We have to do this every time we meditate, and then we are able to wait on God and to accept something for the conscious mind to send down to the deep mind.

So let us say over in the silence the words:

BE STILL FOR I AM WITH YOU

SILENCE

THANKSGIVING

What do we mean by the word God? For hundreds of years He has been thought of as a sort of old man up in the sky and it is very difficult for us to get rid of that mental picture. The truth is that God is everywhere. We say God is in heaven, but heaven is everywhere. As Elizabeth Barrett Browning says:

> "Earth's crammed with heaven
> And every common bush afire with God."

If you go back to the Old Testament you will find that same thought:

> "Am I a God at hand, says the Lord, and not a God far off? Do I not fill heaven and earth?" (Jer. 23. 23).

> "Holy, Holy, Holy, is the Lord of Hosts, the whole earth is full of His glory" (Is. 6. 3).

In the New Testament there are constant references to God's life being everywhere.

> "One God and Father of us all, who is above all and through all and in all" (Eph. 4. 6).

> "In Him we live and move and have our being" (Acts 17. 28).

In preparing for meditation, we begin by thinking about God and the reality of His life everywhere and within everything and always around us and within us. Then we drop the thinking and in the silence allow that knowledge of God to sink deeply into the mind. That really is meditation, not the thinking.

We need to learn to use not only our conscious mind but the deeper part of our mind, the subconscious and the unconscious. We think with the conscious mind and whatever we think about deeply is impressed upon the subconscious mind. The subconscious mind works automatically to express whatever is impressed upon it, so what we give the mind to work on affects the quality of our personality. If our conscious mind dwells on thoughts of peace, joy and love, then our subconscious mind will bring these things out into our life. If we have thoughts of fear, anger and hatred, the subconscious mind will bring these out; it does not pick and choose. It will bring out good or bad, whatever is impressed upon it. "As we think, so we become."

In the unconscious mind we keep what are almost like records of things we do not think about at all, things buried so deep that we are unable to recall them with our conscious mind. For instance the things that happened to us in the very early years of childhood are clearly recorded in our unconscious mind, and so are the emotions attached to whatever happened to us then. If we went through some very frightening experience we would have that recorded and with it all the feelings of fear that we went through.

In meditation we learn to choose thoughts and desires of the highest quality and to impress them on the subconscious mind.

BE STILL AND KNOW MY JOY WITHIN

SILENCE

THANKSGIVING

It is very important to still the conscious mind so that we can drop these truths deeper and deeper into the mind. Thus, meditation fills the mind with truth and melts away wrong ideas. As we persevere, the truth reaches right down into the deepest part of the mind, the unconscious mind. Even fears and negative thoughts buried deep in the unconscious mind can be dissolved by meditation.

It is very important for our deep unconscious mind to be healed because it is there that we store so much that is harmful to us. When something unpleasant or frightening happens to us we have a tendency to push the memory of it down into the unconscious mind, so we have an awful lot of misery, fear, resentment and anxiety buried there. The trouble is that these negative feelings do not always remain buried; they tend to push their way up later on in life, and are often the cause of both mental and physical illness.

A man I knew had a very bad skin disease and he was helped by a psychiatrist who used one of the drugs which brings back memories buried deep in the unconscious mind. This drug brought out the fact that when he was a tiny baby he used to scream at night. His cot was beside his parents' bed but his father could not stand the screaming so he would pick him up out of his warm cot and put him into another bedroom, into a cold bed in a cold room. Although he had no memory of it the record was stored up and caused him to have a terrible resentment against his father. The resentment was not his fault; you cannot blame him for his unconscious reaction to his father's unkindness, but emotion has a tremendous effect on the body and on its chemical composition: and this man's unconscious resentment of his father was the underlying cause of his skin disease.

So the deep unconscious part of the mind is very important and the negative thoughts and feelings which have gone down into it remain there for a very long time unless something is done about changing them.   This can be done by meditation, by dropping into the deepest part of the mind something positive which will dissolve what is negative.

We do not usually meditate on sentences which come directly from the Bible, such as "Be still and know that I am God" because we know the Bible too well and have already made up our minds what the words mean.   Instead we take one quality of God's life such as His peace, His joy or His love. As we drop these Words of Life into the deep mind we then find that we are being changed.   Meditation changes us in vital ways and it is what we *are* that is an influence on other people, much more than what we say to them.   As we meditate on the love of God our attitude to other people changes.   It is not anything you can watch growing, but you begin to find that you are getting on better with those whom you have found difficult or who used to rub you up the wrong way and perhaps made you unkind in the things you said or thought.

In the same way someone who has worried a lot begins to find that he is much calmer and that a sense of peace has come to him; someone who has had fits of misery finds that meditation on joy is gradually changing him.   You will perhaps not notice the change, but if we grow in a deeper love to God and in a deeper consciousness of His life and work within, we really are beginning to grow into a deeper likeness to God.

So let us take the meditation:

BE STILL AND KNOW MY LOVE WITHIN

SILENCE

THANKSGIVING

Let us go forth in peace.

III Becoming God conscious
BE STILL AND KNOW MY PRESENCE
SILENCE
THANKSGIVING

We have been thinking about the way we use our minds in prayer and of how the subconscious mind reproduces in our lives whatever thoughts and feelings it receives, whether good or bad. So it is very important that we learn to control our thoughts and do not allow bad things to go down into our deep mind. Ezekiel, speaking of evil, says: "On that day thoughts will come into your mind, and you will devise an evil scheme" (38. 10), and he points out that evil begins in the mind and then is expressed through the body.

If we fill our minds with evil our lives will express evil, but in the same way if we fill our minds with what is good our lives will express good. When we meditate on the qualities of God's character we begin to find, after some time of perseverance, meditating every day, that we are actually growing in these qualities, we are calmer in all that we do, we are easier to live with; meditation is changing us.

When we meditate we are not concerned about self, we do not try to stir up any nice feelings, nor try to do anything. We just repeat the words over in a sentence, not trying to push them down, not trying to concentrate but just letting go and relaxing, letting the words sink deeply.

Do not try to think about the words and what exactly they mean. Let the Holy Spirit within "Take of the things of Christ and show them unto us". The more we can let *God* do and the less we do ourselves the more He will be able to teach us. So "*let go and let God*". Just be calm and learn to wait on God.

BE STILL AND KNOW THAT MY SPIRIT
IS WITHIN YOU

THANKSGIVING

When you are learning to meditate it is a good thing to notice the clock and to set yourself a limited time, just two minutes to begin with. Do not force yourself to go on to longer periods, it will come in time and even when you learn to keep quiet for longer periods do not be afraid of shortening the time again if you begin to find it difficult to keep your mind from wandering.

But it is well worth persevering because meditation is such a reasonable process. Through meditation, people are healed of all sorts of diseases; healed, not only of illness but of a great many things such as fear and anxiety. All these things can be changed because the deep mind expresses everything that is impressed upon it. If you think thoughts of fear you are likely to go on having further thoughts of fear. If you think thoughts of depression and misery you will impress these thoughts on the deep mind and the mind will express them in the body and in the character. Whatever is impressed on the deep mind comes out, and comes out more and more vehemently the deeper it is impressed. It is rather like what happens when we hear something funny. We begin with a smile and if it is really funny we laugh out loud, and if it is funnier still and goes even deeper we roar with laughter. So it is with fear: if a thought of fear comes into your mind you begin to feel afraid, but if the fear is impressed more deeply on your mind it begins to affect your body and you go white in the face and tremble. The more deeply ideas are impressed on the mind the greater is their effect.

The Holy Spirit is not a mind and it is not anything physical within—it is the Spirit of God, His spirit of love, goodness, righteousness and so on. If we think of these things and meditate on them so that they are impressed on our deep mind they will gradually fill our whole mind, leaving no room for feelings of fear and anxiety.

But do we always choose our thoughts and refuse to think about things which are unpleasant, hurtful and negative? We all have a great tendency to dwell on unpleasant things, and this is true of all of us, you and me. When something unpleasant happens to us we think a great deal about it, and the more we think about it, the more we impress it on the subconscious mind, the more that mind works within us to continue what is unpleasant. For instance, someone who has a headache tends to tell everyone about it and to grumble and complain about it. Unless he stops talking about it, going over and over his painful symptoms, he will impress his subconscious mind with thoughts of pain and then the subconscious mind, because it works automatically, will start working to produce more painful symptoms.

Probably many of you have had experiences of this kind and find you have got into the habit of talking about them. I wish we could think of something else to say, when we meet people, instead of "How are you?", which encourages them to start talking about their ailments.

The aim of meditation is to train us to be God-conscious at all times; then, however unpleasant our illness may be, we centre our minds, not upon the condition we wish that we could get rid of, and what is really evil, but upon God and on His healing power. It takes a great deal of perseverance to do this, but if we train ourselves by meditation to think positively we shall be able to triumph over problems of this kind.

So the secret of living triumphantly is to learn, quite consciously, to fill our deep mind with thoughts that are good, thoughts of God's life always at work within us.

So let us take the meditation

I WILL REJOICE THAT THOU ART EVER AT WORK WITHIN ME

SILENCE

THANKSGIVING

IV Fear

PRAISE THE LORD, OH MY SOUL,
PRAISE THE LORD

SILENCE

THANKSGIVING

We have been thinking about the importance of being positive in our thoughts and of how destructive negative thoughts can be. Recently I heard from a woman who was quite overwhelmed by her fears and anxieties. Her letter was seven or eight pages long, all filled with the feelings that she has about herself. She ended up by saying she was afraid she might commit suicide. By writing in this way, going over and over the problems and difficulties of her life, just poring over them, she was filling her mind with them, with them and with nothing else. And, as we know, thoughts which are impressed deeply upon the mind inevitably come out into expression, either in the body or in our circumstances.

You have only to think of the way fear can become completely obsessive. When I was a boy of about nine I was wakened up in the middle of the night by the sound of somebody knocking on our front door. I went to the window to tell the person I was coming downstairs and saw that it was a policeman. "Your house is on fire", he shouted. "Come out quickly." I hurried to waken my parents and, as I opened my bedroom door, a cloud of smoke filled my room. I got to my father and mother and woke them, then they woke the rest of the family, and we were all out of the house in about five minutes. We discovered later that the fire had started just close to the gas meter so there was the chance of a very big fire and we might not have got out.

For at least three years after that I never slept through the night without going downstairs to make sure that everything was all right. The fear of fire had absolutely obsessed me: it had gone down so deeply into the subconscious mind that I not only had feelings of fear but felt impelled to go down in the cold, night after night, to convince myself that all was well.

Negative thoughts are tremendously strong, but so too are positive thoughts and, just as there are limitless possibilities of what can happen when we store negative thoughts, so there are limitless possibilities of what can happen when we think positively. We have the power of choice, we can choose what thoughts go down into our minds. If we choose thoughts of joy, peace, beauty, truth and goodness, these will come out into expression.

OPEN OUR EYES, DEAR LORD, TO THY LIFEGIVING SPIRIT WITHIN US

SILENCE

THANKSGIVING

If we are to have this positive attitude towards life, we must first of all get rid of all self concern, of our nagging fear lest we fail in what we have to do. For not only are joy and peace qualities of the Holy Spirit, but so also are capacity and capability. The power of the Holy Spirit within us is not something pious but is a faculty of our life: it is available to us for the ordinary everyday things of life. Religion and life are not separate from one another.

Even people with no belief in God at all, if they could realise that they have a power within them which can become active and increase their ability to do whatever they have to do, would find that this power was there, that it was real. But if we are to know the power of God's life within us, we have to learn to be selfless. After watching a programme on television about China I went on watching because a man came on to play the piano. He began to play Chopin and it absolutely thrilled me, not simply because it was Chopin whose music always thrills me and he played so beautifully;

but what interested me so much was to see his absolute concentration and complete freedom from self-centredness. At the end of each piece he came to himself, smiled and bowed to the audience, but while he was playing there was absolutely nothing of self, and the result was that the music absolutely thrilled the people in the audience. We have to lose ourselves if we are to bring out the capacity that is in us.

So when you have something important to do, try to get into the way of waiting on God. In order to become deeply aware of God's presence, it is not necessary to go away by yourself. Wherever we may be we can be conscious of His power within, which will enable us to do what we have to do with far greater capacity than we had ever expected of ourselves.

Christians ought to be the most capable people in the world, people with the most influential characters. We are not really Christians until we have learned to let this power within come out into expression.

THY LIFE WITHIN IS QUICKENING EVERY FACULTY OF MY BEING

SILENCE

THANKSGIVING

V *The two aims of meditation*
LET ME BE AWARE OF THY SPIRIT WITHIN ME

THANKSGIVING

There are two great aims in meditation and we must keep the two aims in balance. The first aim is to learn to know the reality of God's life *within* us, and we do this by meditating on the qualities of His character, such as His love, His joy, His peace.

The second aim is to learn to know that God's life is *around* us, always working to express itself in and through the whole creation. As we meditate on this thought we come to realise that we are fellow workers with God in His purpose for the world.

We must not forget either of these two aims. If we were to use the first kind of meditation only, trying to develop our own spiritual life, it could mean becoming turned in on self. Nor can we use just the second kind of meditation because we can only become fellow workers with God by learning to know Him and to be aware of the power of His life within us.

If I am filled with the love of God I am bound to express this love in my relationships with other people. The love of God builds up the right kind of relationships, not only between us and those we meet day by day, but also between all the people in the world. We find that as we learn to know God and to work with Him, the world seems to take on a new great meaning. By training ourselves to meditate we can make a contribution towards God's purpose for the world. Realise this in the silence of this meditation, "My servant art thou". Realise that our Lord is saying that to you, then ask yourself: "Am I His servant? Am I really helping Him, His spirit and life in the world, and helping other people to become His servants?"

MY SERVANT ART THOU

THANKSGIVING

Now although meditation teaches us that we are fellow workers with God and that we have His life and His power within us, this does not mean that we are trying to escape all difficulties. It does not mean that everything is going to be easy for us. After all we are fellow workers with Christ and, if we are really united with Him, we shall have to share in His sufferings. He is the light of the world working to overcome the darkness. His purpose is to express His life and His love in the whole creation, and it is a long job.

During our Lord's life on earth this purpose cost Him a great deal, eventually it cost Him the agony and the disappointment of the Cross. And, if we are going to be fellow workers with Him, working to change the world and to bring the power of His Holy Spirit into evidence in human relationships, it is going to cost us a great deal. We begin with the fact that we have got to persevere in meditation, that is part of the price we have to pay. It is part of a disciplined life that finds time for the really important things. The values we seek are the values of the Kingdom of God which is to come on earth. As fellow workers with Christ our aim is that His righteousness, His love and the goodness of His life may be expressed in the life of the whole human race.

HELP US, DEAR LORD, TO HUNGER AND THIRST FOR THY KINGDOM WITH ITS RIGHTEOUSNESS ON EARTH

SILENCE

THANKSGIVING

VI   God the creator

You will find, when you become more practised, that as well as meditating when you can be quiet for a while, you can meditate at odd times during the day.   You will find that you can meditate while waiting for the kettle to boil or when you are on the way to work or to see someone.   Meditating about people you are going to see, or who are coming to see you, will very often have its effect on your whole attitude towards them.

As we take our first meditation, let us think of God being at work not only within us and around us but working to express His life throughout the whole of creation.

THOU OH LORD ART IN THE MIDST OF US

SILENCE

THANKSGIVING

The Bible begins by telling us that God created the whole universe.   The first chapters of Genesis are not a historical or scientific account of creation—they were not even the first part of the Bible to be written—but they do suggest a progressive, creative activity.   We can trace it all through the Bible, this idea of God's purpose being worked out in a creation which slowly works towards the Kingdom of God.   We are not led to expect that the progress of God's purpose will be by any steady or sudden overcoming of evil, but that God has been at work, is now and always will be at work to overcome evil and to perfect all (Matt. 24. 9-28).

I do not think we have got too sure a hold of that truth, that creation was not made perfect all at once but that God is still at work in His creation.   He is everywhere and always at work.   Creation is something that has progressed from early beginnings millions of years ago and is still progressing towards the time that Jesus looked forward to, the time when everything on earth would become as it is in heaven.   It is He who taught us to pray: "Thy Kingdom come on earth as it is in heaven".

Creation is a unity—we are very slow to realise the unity of the whole of creation—and God is working within it towards the ultimate purpose of expressing His own life in all.

Creation is progressive, like the growth of a tree. An apple tree does not start by showing what its true nature is—its flowers and fruit come late in its history. As the tree grows, the roots and the stem, the branches and the leaves all make their contribution to the ultimate flowering of the tree. So it is with creation. In its early stages there were just the mountains, seas and skies to express the beauty of God, then came life, plants and animals able to express much more of God. Eventually when man came he was capable of expressing a great deal more of God. The whole creation is gradually building up to the time when man will come to his full flowering, when not only will every bush be "afire with God" but every human being afire with the spirit of God. When these qualities begin to come out into expression, men and nations will learn to live together in love, justice and righteousness. That is the purpose which we see unfolding in creation.

But so often when we hear people talking about the purpose of God we get overwhelmed by the idea of His bigness and we feel quite helpless. However can we do anything to fill the earth with the glory of God? What can we do?

The only answer is "You can be what God wants you to be, and it is what you are that affects other people around you". If every Christian in the world was growing day by day in love towards other people, in care for others, if every Christian longed to see God's righteousness expressed in the world, what influence they would have! It is not anything that anyone does, but their influence which makes an amazing difference. I do not think we realise nearly as much as we ought what an immense influence we could have if only our thinking was on the right lines all the time. There is no need to tell people whether we are Christians or not, but if our whole minds were saturated with a consciousness of God's Holy Spirit within, that consciousness would spread. It would spread from person to person until the beauty and the goodness and the love of God were expressed in the character of the whole human race.

Meditation teaches us to realise the quality of God's life not only within us but within the whole creation. In the last chapter we used the meditation "My servant art thou"; now let us take the whole sentence from Isaiah 49. 3.

MY SERVANT ART THOU IN WHOM I WILL BE GLORIFIED

SILENCE

THANKSGIVING

But where do we see the glory of God? When we look round at the people we meet day by day, when we read our newspapers, which give only what is negative and unhappy, it does not seem as though God is at work. Man is cruel, selfish and unjust. St. Paul recognised the fact. "All men have sinned and have fallen short of the glory of God." That is the truth, for God's work is not yet finished; but the great thing to realise is that He *is at* work all the time.

We believe that Christ is dealing with the sin and evil of the world by taking it on Himself and overcoming it. His life is in the world and in us, working day by day to redeem what is evil.

This aim of learning to know God in the midst of His creation was the aim of much of Our Lord's teaching about the Kingdom of Heaven. If you were to take away all His teaching about the Kingdom you would cut out a large number of His parables and a great deal more of His teaching. St. Paul speaks of the whole creation groaning and travailing in pain as in a great birth, waiting for the promise of God to be fulfilled. It is that purpose of God which we need to have continually in our minds if we are to glorify Him and work with Him making His purpose known to all.

I WILL STIR UP IN THEE KNOWLEDGE OF MY LIFE AT WORK WITHIN THE WHOLE CREATION

SILENCE

THANKSGIVING

VII   *The spirit needs the right conditions*
I AM ETERNAL GOODNESS WITHIN YOU

SILENCE

THANKSGIVING

Meditation is very much concerned with bringing out the best that is in us—and there is a great deal more good within each one of us than we ever realise. William Law, the seventeenth century mystic, wrote: "There is, in every man born into the world, a seed of divine life in which are all the riches of eternity". But this seed of divine life has to be brought out into expression.

Think of the life of an acorn.   Every single acorn has within it the possibility of growing into a great forest oak in all its grandeur and splendour.   In the same way every single human being has within him the power to grow into the likeness of Christ.

The acorn will not grow into a forest oak unless it is given the right kind of physical surroundings—if you put it in your desk it just dries up, nothing happens, but if you put it into the good soil and it has rain and sunshine it will grow and begin to characterise all the potential within it.   It will grow towards its ultimate perfection and purpose.   The same goes for man to a great extent.   He needs food, warmth and so on, but because human beings are much further on in God's creation we need something more in order to develop our full potential—we need knowledge of God.   The acorn must be rooted to one place, but there is something far more important, and that is that we have a mind.   The acorn has no mind, nor any choice, but we have a choice, we have a mind, and we can choose the kind of thoughts that we fill it with.

If we are to begin to characterise the potentialities for greatness which are within us we must feed our minds with the right kind of thoughts. If the seed of divine life which is within us is to come out into full expression we need to become aware of the qualities of God's life already within us, of His righteousness, joy, peace, courage, strength, beauty and love. This is the aim of meditation, not to put into us something we have not got, but to draw out from us God's infinite spirit, containing "all the riches of eternity".

LET THE INFINITE POSSIBILITIES WITHIN US COME OUT INTO EXPRESSION

SILENCE

THANKSGIVING

Think for a moment of this infinite spirit of God which is within every one of us. It is this spirit which created the universe and has been working in it for millions of years. It is this spirit which brought Christ into the world and which is working now to express God's character in and through the life of the human race and in all human relationships. God's spirit is the spirit of righteousness, that is of love and justice, and therefore is adequate to overcome war, hatred between nations, greediness which brings starvation, in fact every kind of evil. Our Lord speaks of it: "Seek ye first the Kingdom of God and His righteousness". It is our purpose in life as Christians to build up this spirit in all human relationships.

But it is so easy to forget that God's spirit is always with us and in us, so easy to be influenced by the negative thinking of the world. Yet if we really had this deeper knowledge of the power of God's Holy Spirit within us we could live our lives at their best. But so often we fill our minds with negative thoughts and feelings of fear and inferiority. "I can't do this" or "I'm afraid to do that" and we begin to think of people who can do things much better than we can. We become depressed and faithless, living as though God did not exist. So we need to meditate on the reality of the Holy Spirit within us and to get this thought very deep into our

minds before the realisation of His presence comes naturally
to us. But it will come, if we persevere, and we shall find as
we go on that God's spirit is able to overcome all problems and
difficulties. It is, in fact, adequate to all our needs.

I WILL TRUST IN THEE
HOLY SPIRIT WITHIN

SILENCE

THANKSGIVING

VIII The power of the risen Christ

It is very easy to let the mind wander off on some aspect of the meditation, or in some quite different direction; almost anything can distract us. But when we have made some progress it is quite a good thing to have distractions occasionally because they help us to learn how to deal with them. If it is music, we can try to enter into the rhythm of it and get beyond the distraction. When I was in London we often used to meditate with the sound of jazz coming from next door or with the noise of an automatic drill in the road outside.

Another difficulty that people find, particularly at first, is that they have to struggle with sleepiness. If you find that you get sleepy do not be bothered about it—have your sleep out and if there is a little time left then go on with the meditation. There is no need to be concerned because you will soon learn to get beyond that. Never blame yourself for it.

So let us try to be quiet as we take for our first meditation the words

I WOULD BE ALIVE TO THY LIFE WITHIN ME

SILENCE

THANKSGIVING

The Christian religion is a way of life lived in the conscious-ness of Christ's life within, and yet most people live as though life were just one thing after another, every day much the same as another. How different it would be if every Christian really believed that he had Christ's life within him.

Our Lord often spoke of His unity with His Father; "I and My Father are one"; and he gave us the assurance that His life would be in us. "I will not leave you comfortless, I will come to you." Through meditation we can learn to know the reality of this truth.

St. Paul, talking about the life of our Lord being within us, says: "The Christ you have to deal with is not a weak person, outside you but a tremendous power inside you . . . You ought to know by this time that Christ is in you, unless you are not real Christians at all". II Cor. 13 (J. B. Phillips' translation).

St. Paul goes on "We are glad to be weak if it means that you are strong, but our ambition for you is true Christian maturity". We shall only become really mature Christians as we grow up into Christ's likeness and learn to know the fulness of His life within us. In meditation the aim is not just healing, nor just having deeper spiritual experience. We are not looking for what people speak of as "uplift", what we are aiming at is becoming more whole in the sense of becoming more fully like God, growing into what St. Paul speaks of as "the measure of the stature of Christ". "This is life eternal, that they may know the Father and Jesus Christ whom He has sent."

In meditation we try to let go all self concern and wait on God, just allowing the words to sink deeply into the mind, realising that because God is real He will make Himself known to us.

THAT IN MY DAILY LIFE I MAY KNOW THY POWER WITHIN

SILENCE

THANKSGIVING

This life of God is not something that we can see. A mother talking to her two small children, spoke of God's life being everywhere and in every person they met. Janice looked thoughtful. "Is God in me?" she asked. "Yes." "Is God in Peter?" "Yes." "Oh," she exclaimed, "I would like to cut him open and see what God is like".

It is the same with the acorn. Although it is true that "There is an oak tree in every acorn", yet if we cut it open we should not find a miniature tree. So although we cannot see "life", God's creative life is there in each one of us and therefore the potentiality or the possibility of something so much greater than we tend to think.

Although Jesus had died on the Cross, to His disciples He was not just a person they had known in the past. They did not merely talk about Him and the parables that He taught and the works of healing He had done, but they preached Jesus, that He IS the Christ. They realised that He had brought the life of God's Kingdom on earth. They had seen the power of it in His own life and when He rose from the dead they had the assurance of His life and His power within them.

For our final meditation on the theme of power let us take

THAT WE MAY KNOW HIM AND THE POWER OF HIS RISEN LIFE WITHIN US

SILENCE

THANKSGIVING

IX   *The difficulty of putting away false ideas*

THY LIFE IS A CONTINUING PURPOSE
AT WORK WITHIN US

SILENCE

THANKSGIVING

There ought to be great expectation arising out of our faith in the indwelling spirit of God, but the trouble is that we find it extraordinarily difficult to believe that God's spirit is within us.   For years and years we have been taught that God is up above the bright blue sky, that He is far away. I wonder whether we realise that this idea of God brings with it a carelessness.   God is so far away that He does not think anything about us.   Perhaps, as Elijah taunted the prophets of Baal, He has gone hunting, perhaps He is away having a meal, or is asleep or something.   We find it very difficult to put away our wrong ideas about God, even though we know perfectly well that they are false ideas.

When my son and his family returned to this country from Africa they brought with them the African girl who had been helping to look after the children.   She stayed with the family for some years and we all looked on her as one of the family. She was a very good Christian.   She decided she wanted to become a nurse and so she trained for her S.R.N. and then went on to do her maternity training.   She spent quite a lot of her holidays with us.   One day when she was with us I went out to church early in the morning; it was in the middle of summer and it was very hot; it had been hot all night. I happened to look back at the house and saw that her window was tight shut.   When I came back for breakfast, I said to her: "Why do you have your window shut in this hot weather?" and she replied with a sort of shudder: "I would not dare to have it open".   I tried to get her to tell me why,

but she was terribly shy about this.   Then at last it came out.
"I am afraid that if I left it open an evil spirit might come
and take me back to Africa."   There, underneath all the
civilised thoughts that had come to her living in England,
underneath all the belief she had come to about Christianity
and the church and her Christian life, deep down in her mind
were the thoughts that she had had as a small child in Africa,
pagan thoughts.

What thoughts are there deep in your mind?   I think
many of us still have a tremendous lot of wrong ideas about
God deep down in our minds and the only way of pushing
out these wrong ideas is by pushing in the truth, the real truth
that God is with us and within us—always.

MY GOD I THANK THEE THAT THOU ART
ALWAYS WITHIN ME

SILENCE

THANKSGIVING

Although we have learned that God's spirit is within every
human being, whether they are Christians or not, do we really
believe this with our whole heart?   We may believe that
God's spirit is within us, but do we really realise that His
spirit is also within every single person that we meet?   It may
not be apparent, there may be no sign of it that we can find,
but it is always there, within.   Before it can be manifested
it may need to be drawn out—and that is what every
Christian ought to be doing all the time—learning how to
draw out from others the expression of God's Holy Spirit in
their lives.   There are endless opportunities for us to draw
out this power in others if only we have sufficient faith and
courage.

There are infinite possibilities in every single person—far
greater possibilities than any of us realise—possibilities which
can be brought out into expression.

You know how often we get disappointed in someone, how often we wonder at people doing such dreadful things, and yet there are infinite possibilities of good even in people who seem to be quite hopeless. There is always far more good in such people than we can ever see and it helps them enormously if we think well of them, if we think of what they can become rather than of what they seem to be. To have real hope of people is half way towards being able to help them.

There is a deep link between our thoughts and other people's minds and you cannot keep what you think about a person from him. So if you think negatively of a person you hinder him from becoming what he could become, but if you think good thoughts for him you help him to achieve that good.

HELP US TO HOLD FAST TO THE BLESSED HOPE OF FULNESS OF LIFE

SILENCE

THANKSGIVING

X *Peace*

I think it is a good thing to come back again and again to the simple meditations on the qualities of God's character. So while we are trying to relax, to let go anything we are worrying about, any strain or tension, we can hold in our minds the words:

MY PEACE I GIVE UNTO YOU

SILENCE

THANKSGIVING

We all have our own ideas of what peace is like, but I think that most people think of peace as an escape from some sort of turmoil. We tend to think of it as the sense of relief we feel when we are saved from some difficulty or opposition or as something that follows disturbance. When the children are finally settled in bed a tired mother rests back in her chair and says "What peace!"

But God's peace is something quite different and we can only learn to have it if we listen to His teaching. "Peace I leave with you, My peace I give unto you, not as the world giveth give I unto you". We can only learn it if we are very humble and receptive, if we are prepared to try and get really quiet and in that way to allow ourselves to know His peace. As we wait, the Holy Spirit teaches us. The trouble is that we are generally unready to learn to experience the peace of God; we very seldom get quiet enough to experience that inner quietness, a quietness of the mind and of the soul.

However often we meditate on peace and however much we learn about it, the Holy Spirit always has something more to teach us. We do not try to imagine what the Holy Spirit is teaching us, we just try to be alive to the living God within us. If He teaches us then we shall know it.

I WILL BE STILL AND LEARN OF THEE,
SPIRIT OF PEACE WITHIN

THANKSGIVING

Once we have learned to know the peace of God we shall find that we can call upon it and become aware of it whenever we need it. When we have to face something difficult and we feel inadequate to it, we only have to realise that the peace of God is within us and that in that peace all the power of God is at work. This gives us tremendous strength and confidence.

But we have to get away from the idea that peace is a matter of escape. Our Lord found His peace in the midst of His difficulties. It was always there with Him and He was conscious of it all the time. It came from the consciousness that "I and my Father are one". The presence of God was so real to Him that it gave Him a confidence and a calmness so that He could say: "I do nothing by myself . . .".

That is the kind of peace we need, peace which comes from union with God and the complete sense of the reliability of God's Holy Spirit within. Once we come to accept the truth that this peace is always within us we shall find in our own experience that we are no longer giving way to worry as we used to do. Instead of feeling at a loss to know what to do we simply get quiet for a moment and become conscious of God's presence and of His wisdom and calmness.

The sense of peace we experience when we learn to know God's peace is not a *feeling* of calmness but the *knowledge* of the complete power and adequacy of God to meet all our needs. "In quietness and confidence shall be your strength."

TEACH US TO KNOW THY PEACE WITHIN THAT WE MAY BE STRENGTHENED WITH THY STRENGTH

SILENCE

THANKSGIVING

XI Entering into God's purpose for the world

GIVE US KNOWLEDGE, DEAR LORD, KNOWLEDGE OF THY PURPOSE

SILENCE

THANKSGIVING

We need, in all our meditations, to be seeking a deeper knowledge of God. Surely it is what our Lord meant: "This is life eternal, that they may know the Father and Jesus Christ whom He sent". As the knowledge of God deepens within us we enter into the thoughts of God and of what His purposes are for ourselves and for the whole world. There is no selfishness about our prayers and our meditations, we are not seeking pleasure for ourselves, nor even holiness just for ourselves, we are seeking to know God's purpose for the whole creation.

God is dependent upon us for our co-operation if His purpose for the world is to be achieved. We have got to begin by thinking about it. After all, is there anything we ever do without thinking? If you do not think before you go out shopping you will not bring back the things you need. If you do not think about your holiday you will not be ready when the time for it comes. So it is with us if we are to co-operate with God. He has given us minds able to think about Him and to visualise His will for us and for the world.

In our thinking, in our vision of God's world as He means it to be, we need to think of the people in every country of the world as children of God. Every single person ought to be sharing in the wonderful gifts God has given to mankind. We need to be much more aware of the unity of the human race as the family of God and to remember our Lord's command: "Seek ye first the Kingdom of God and His righteousness".

The trouble is that we seem unable to think of God as being

concerned about all the people of the world or about the kind of world we live in. We have neglected the teaching our Lord gave us about His Kingdom, which was to come on earth as it is in Heaven. For too long we have been content with the world as it is. We criticise it sometimes but we do not feel the urgency to do something about the terrible cruelty in the world, the wars, the hunger and the appalling sickness.

While I was thinking about this and our attitude towards the world, I could not help realising that for well over eighty years I have been having three meals a day despite the fact that there are millions of people without even one proper meal a day, and that for a great many years I have had money in the bank although there are people in deep need in so many countries and even here in our own country. Then I could not help thinking also how I have paid taxes for years, and part of that money has gone to buy arms to kill people in different parts of the world. I ask myself, "Where shall I be on the Day of Judgment? Shall I be in what the Bible speaks of as 'Abraham's bosom'—the Kingdom of God, or will this record of my life stand in the way?"

What do we do in face of the conditions of the world? God is working all the time, though He never forces anyone, but He is longing for us to work with Him to change what is wrong in the world. What can we do? We may say: "There is little we can do", but as Christians I think that this ought perhaps to be the most important thing that we think about in prayer. As I said before, prayer is thinking— entering into the thought of God—and thought is the most powerful thing in the world. We never do anything without previous thought. We never so much as move from one part of the room to another without thought. Thought is the beginning of all action.

St. Paul longed to "have the mind of Christ", to have the thoughts of Christ and the desire of Christ's mind. So let us take his prayer as our meditation.

THAT I MAY HAVE THE MIND OF CHRIST

SILENCE

THANKSGIVING

Supposing we really understood that in every single child suffering from starvation it is Jesus Himself who suffers in that child, "Inasmuch as ye have done it unto one of the least of these . . . ye have done it to Me". If that became a really personal thing to us we should begin to do something about it. If the roof of your house begins to leak or the back door blows off in a gale, what do you do? You have got to do something at once. You begin to think how to get the damage repaired. As you think, ideas come into your mind and you get something done. But thinking about it is the first thing. Nothing would happen if you just left the roof leaking and the back door lying outside in the yard.

But the problem has to be really personal. When I was at Cambridge I watched from my window one Guy Fawkes day as students were piling wood on top of a bonfire. They were pulling down garden fences and seizing anything they could get hold of to burn. I thoroughly enjoyed watching them. I saw several of them carrying a bicycle high in the air and they threw is right on top. How I enjoyed seeing it. That is until someone said: "Do you know that is your bicycle?" It became personal to me immediately. Then, quick as life, I thought to myself: "I must run out there", and that led to me rushing out to rescue it.

Nobody is going to do anything very much about the starvation or sickness in the world, about the stopping of wars or the building up of better relationships between the nations, nobody is going to do anything at all about any of these things until there has been very deep thought, and that thinking has got to begin with prayer. We have got to think of the leaders of the nations and pray that they may learn righteousness (justice and love) and bring that into their thinking about the problems of the world. That is a job for the Christian church because a great many of the leaders of the world do not know God at all. But until Christians begin to do something, thinking every single day of those who are in responsible positions and of the people of the nations, nothing will happen. But we have been in darkness —that is why we do not really believe that God is concerned.

LET THY LIGHT SHINE WITHIN ME

Let Thy power and Thy glory and the mightiness of Thy Kingdom become known unto men.

SILENCE

THANKSGIVING

XII *How emotions affect the body*

THY PRESENCE WITHIN IS FULNESS OF LIFE

SILENCE

THANKSGIVING

Our minds ought to be filled with the knowledge of God, but the trouble is that so often they are filled with negative emotions and feelings. It is perfectly possible for us to be swayed and dominated by negative emotions without our realising it at all.

In these days life is very frustrating to most people and because of this sense of frustration there is very often a deep resentment within us which causes bitterness and very often depression. We go about day by day with regrets in our minds and fear of what may be coming and, although this happens again and again, we can be completely unaware of it. We may be aware that something is making us uneasy, that we do not feel at our best, but very often we are not conscious of anything really wrong until suddenly we become ill.

Maybe we get a pain in the back or in some other part of the body or we find that we get indigestion or a cold or a temperature, and as a rule we rush off to the doctor to try to get something to put it right. What we do not do is to stop for a moment to ask ourselves "Why has this come?" "What has been the cause of it?"

Our mental hospitals are full of people who have become ill on account of dis-ease or disharmony in their emotional life. And in our other hospitals there are many patients whose physical illnesses are also the result of causes which are not physical but emotional.

There is a great deal of teaching today about psychosomatic medicine. But, although it is well known that a great deal of illness comes from emotional causes, from emotions deeply buried in the mind, there is very little teaching about how to change these deep emotions. Yet they can be changed.

It is very important for us to realise that, although the negative emotion is evil, it is not sin. It is not something which we choose of our free will, it is something that seems to come to us. These feelings of frustration, fear, anxiety and often great bitterness are very often due to circumstances which simply arise, maybe within the family. When we are under this sort of strain it is bound to have a physical expression of some kind or another. Any emotion whatever that passes through our minds affects the ductless glands in our bodies and the result is that these glands pour chemicals into our blood stream and the whole metabolism of our bodies is changed. Negative emotions can cause things like rheumatism or other kinds of pain or may even be the cause of asthma or other bronchial troubles.

So first of all we have got to train ourselves to be aware of these negative emotions then, through meditation, to meet the situation which has caused us to have feelings like that.

The lack of spiritual wholeness which is the cause of so much illness can be helped by spiritual means, by counteracting negative emotions with the consciousness of God's love, peace and joy, and sometimes of His forgiveness. The life of God is a constant healing work going on within us all the time, and, if we can only make the time day by day to dwell on the positive aspects of God's character, we shall experience the power of God to triumph over illness.

When we have learned to be aware of the evil we must then try to let that evil go. If we meditate in this way we can very often change the whole tone of our physical well-being, the whole tone of our life. I would like you now to take as a meditation

WE THANK THEE THAT ALL DEPRESSION, RESENTMENT AND FEAR ARE BEING MELTED AWAY BY THE INCOMING OF THY LOVE INTO OUR HEARTS AND MINDS

There is the distinct recognition of evil although it is going out and being replaced by the love of God. So let us say this sentence over and over in the silence.

SILENCE

THANKSGIVING

People sometimes resist the idea that they may have, say, resentment within them. Someone who has rheumatoid arthritis very badly may resist the idea that resentment and bitterness could be the cause. They just will not allow themselves to accept the fact and so they go on trying every remedy that is suggested to them, except meditation. They will not attempt to learn meditation because, they feel, that would accuse them of something of which they are ashamed.

We want to remind ourselves, again and again, that these deep feelings are not due to any fault on our part but have come to us as a result of circumstances in our lives. It may possibly be the result of something which happened when we were babies. Whether these feelings are recognised or not they have their effect on the body and, if we hide them, they only go on working deeply within us, causing pain and illness.

We also want to be very clear that these personal emotions can be changed—meditation can change them. We ought to come to our meditations with great expectation, realising that we are meant to express God's character. God is righteousness, that is rightness in relationships, which very often means forgivingness. We do not meditate in this way simply in order to heal our particular pain or illness but because it is part of our training as Christians to learn to call out the infinite love of God into expression.

So as our last meditation let us hold in our minds the thought of God's love and forgivingness.

DEEPEN THY LOVE AND THY FORGIVINGNESS WITHIN US DEAR LORD

SILENCE

THANKSGIVING

XIII   Light

LET THY LIGHT SHINE THROUGH OUR DARKNESS

We all know that light banishes physical darkness.   If we
go into a dark room and turn on the electric light, the darkness
immediately disappears, and in the same way when the
night is over and dawn breaks, the darkness goes.

In this world we are surrounded by darkness which is not
physical, a darkness which needs God's light to banish it.
This light is available to us, but we have to learn how to use
its power.   If we had electricity laid on in the house but did
not switch it on we should still be in darkness just as much as
if we had no electricity.   God's light is like that.   It *is* within
us and we have the apparatus to enable us to use it, but we
need to learn how to use it.

When I speak of the darkness of the world I do not
necessarily mean wickedness or evil, but a darkness of which
we are often unaware.   We are surrounded by the darkness
of negative thoughts and negative feelings, and are affected
by them far more than we realise.   For instance fear, due to
lack of faith, brings instability and loneliness.   That is
darkness.   Frustration very often leads to antagonism.   The
uncertainty of the world and a lack of expectation of something
good affect us in different ways and affect our attitude towards
other people and can make us bitter and lacking in love
towards them.   All this kind of darkness is responsible for
an enormous amount of ill health.

This darkness of negative attitudes and negative feelings
has been pressing on us for years and years and still is pressing
on us all the time.   That is why we need to come back, again
and again, to meditations on light.   God's light, the light of

His character, of His love, joy, goodness, beauty, truth, wisdom and peace dispels the darkness and fills the mind with what is positive. Gradually, as we learn through meditation to let that light shine within us and as we dwell on the thought of its living presence, it enables us to enter into the kind of life that God wants us to live and to experience.

Because we are so tremendously affected by the atmosphere of the world, the atmosphere of darkness, it takes a great deal of perseverance to learn to meditate. It is not something you can hurry, nor is it something which brings any sort of feelings. We just have to go on expecting that light is stealing into the mind and will have its effect, not expecting to have any sort of feelings that show us that this is going on. I think our tendency to expect that we shall either hear something with our ears or experience some uplifting feelings only makes it more difficult for us to learn to meditate. There is no doubt whatever that God communicates with us, but not in words or even in thoughts. God may have spoken to us, may have communicated something to us even though we have had no feelings and have heard nothing. We shall know that He has spoken to us when later on we find ourselves growing in peace and becoming less fussy about things, meeting difficulties more calmly and beginning to find that we have a deeper joy.

But supposing you do have feelings, say, of tremendous peace, do not take too much notice of them. Some people, particularly when they are beginning, say that they have very deep spiritual feelings as a result of meditation, but these are not very important. Von Hügel, who was a very good spiritual director, wrote in letters to his niece: "Be silent about great things that seem to happen to you, the feelings of devotion and feelings of calmness and peace when you have been meditating. Let them grow inside you, and whatever you do, never discuss them with anyone else. Discussion is so limiting and distracting. If you let them grow inside you they will begin to express themselves in your life".

I think that advice is good because if the peace of God does begin to express itself in your life other people with whom you have to deal will be influenced by it and be helped by it. But if you talk about it to other people they will only think it is a nine day wonder and it will almost certainly feed your pride, which is certainly something to be avoided. So you just go on trying to let go all self-concern, waiting on God, knowing that He is real, and allowing Him to work within you to bring His own life and character into expression. Therefore by being still and filling our minds with the light of His own light and character we enable God to do what He wants to do with us.

MY LIFE IS AT WORK WITHIN YOU
REJOICE AND BE GLAD

SILENCE

THANKSGIVING

It is a very good thing to allow yourself to rejoice at God's presence. Light is His activity in all the world. We do not often express our joy in our worship—some hymns do, but a great many are very lacking in joy. It is good for us simply to be still and let the heart rejoice in the goodness of God, and to do that not merely when we are feeling that we want to express that joy, but to do it sometimes when we are feeling rather dull. God does not depend upon our feelings, but it is a good thing to let our feelings go, especially in a positive way.

We need the light of God's love and God's spirit and in meditation we can allow it to sink into us and so help us to become much more positive in our thoughts and feelings. The higher the quality of the thought that we allow to enter into the mind, the higher the quality and the more brilliant will the light within become. This is not imagination, we have got the power of God's Holy Spirit within us. "Ye know Him for He dwelleth with you and shall be in you" . . .

This can be brought into expression in our life and if it is, then we will begin to realise the almost limitless power that is within because of this spirit of God within.

But we are so tempted to forget and to live as if God did not exist. So we must persevere with meditation on these deep positive aspects of God's character.

WAKEN IN ME THE POWER OF THY HOLY SPIRIT WHICH IS ALWAYS ADEQUATE TO MY NEED

SILENCE

THANKSGIVING

XIV *Evolution*

HOLY SPIRIT WITHIN, MAKE THYSELF KNOWN TO US

SILENCE

THANKSGIVING

When we start talking to anyone about religion we are almost bound to begin by making some sort of statement about God. But the trouble is the word "God" so often conveys entirely wrong ideas.

How can we teach the truth about God? Our faith and our whole religion obviously must be based on what is true. A basic truth which we all acknowledge is the fact of the universe. We all know that we live in a world and a universe and that we are a part of it. That is something that everybody believes in.

The next important thing to teach people is that although we are part of the universe we are a very late part in the whole process by which the universe came into being. Man did not exist in the early stages of creation and when we begin to think of the steps, one by one, which led up to his development, it is difficult not to think that there is some purpose in creation.

Julian Huxley said: "Every step in the whole process of evolution has led up to the production of man" and so there has been progress towards something greater than creation, or to something that is bigger than that which has appeared first of all. And it is the end product of a process which is always the most important thing. You may see all sorts of things in the process of production in a big firm of car manufacturers but it is only when the final motor car comes out complete that you see what all the little bits have contributed towards.

De Chardin says: "You do not judge the river by the little muddy streams in the mountains thousands of miles away. You do not judge the beauty of the river by them but by the completed and perfected river that runs out of the estuary". So we think of man coming at the end of a long process and man revealing far more of the purpose of the universe than any of the earlier steps towards it.

We expect to find in our human nature very much more of the purpose behind creation. So we believe that in every human being there is revealed to us something of the creator. In Christ, whom we think of as the most perfect human being who has ever lived we see human nature at its best, the crown of creation.

TEACH ME TO KNOW THY CREATIVE LIFE AT WORK WITHIN ME

SILENCE

THANKSGIVING

This creative life is what we mean by God. The prophet, Habakkuk spoke about God as the "incorruptible spirit which is in all things", and when Isaiah says: "Holy, Holy, Holy, Lord God of Hosts, the earth is full of Thy glory" he sees the earth as something that reveals the beauty of God. It is in the whole world that we see the purpose of God, that is expressing it stage by stage until at last His life is expressed in human terms and is the fullest expression of all.

Meditation is the way in which we learn to know the character of God. We do not meditate on the word "God" which is only a symbol and does not really express anything of His character. That is why we have to split up our ideas of God into words of life—we cannot grasp them all at once. So we meditate on words which really express His character— His love, His truth, His beauty and so on. God is not just an idea of love or of truth; He *is* love, He *is* truth. As we

meditate day by day we gradually come to a knowledge of
God Himself and of His creative life at work within us.

GIVE ME KNOWLEDGE OF THYSELF, DEAR LORD,
ALWAYS WITHIN

SILENCE

THANKSGIVING

XV Grief

MY SOUL WAITS IN STILLNESS UPON THEE

SILENCE

THANKSGIVING

We have been thinking about the way in which our thoughts affect us; they affect not only our characters but also our bodies. We know that when we feel disturbed or thwarted, poisons created by our glands pour into the blood stream. What can we do to increase the natural forces which are working within us for health?

What sort of emotions cause pain and ill health? There are some things that are perfectly clear and one of them is that grief is very often the cause of illness. Many times I have found someone ill in bed with asthma, gasping their life away, really in danger of death, and when I have talked to them have found out that they have been through some great grief and have been keeping this grief to themselves, turning it over and over in their minds. I have found that once I have been able to help them to bring out their grief, to talk about it, they begin to recover from their asthma.

I was once asked to see a woman and all I was told about her was that she had had an accident, her face had been torn open and the scar had now healed up. But she had terrible pain in the scar, down the side of her face and in her eye. When she came to see me she told me she had been attacked by an Alsatian. So I asked her about the accident, what had led up to it, what exactly happened, and she told me all about it. When I said to her: "What happened afterwards, when you were getting better, when the wound was healing up?" she told me a few things then she started to cry. Suddenly she said, "And then my husband died". I pressed her to tell me all the details of his death and she told me that he had just come in from work and sat down for a cup of tea when he fell back dead in his chair. When she had told me all about his death, I still pressed her to tell me about his funeral and she went into tremendous detail and told me everything. Then quite suddenly she drew herself up very stiffly and said: "I cannot think why ever I told you about this, I have never spoken about it ever since it happened, not to anyone before". I said to her: "Are you surprised then that your grief has been trying to find an outlet and that it has gone to the weakest place, the scar on your face?"

From the time she got all that out, had shared her grief with somebody else, the scar ceased to hurt her. There was someone in the village where she lived who had a meditation group which she was able to join, but without the meditation she would have recovered once she had got her grief out.

But there are many people today suffering ill health through grief even though they have been able to talk about it. What they need to learn is to get the love of God deep into their hearts and the awareness that those whom they have lost are with God and are therefore very close to them still. Once they can get that assurance their health will begin to improve. It is the same with many kinds of emotion and there are so many people who are needing to learn meditation in order that they may experience wholeness through a deeper awareness of the love of God.

HELP US TO HOLD FAST TO THE BLESSED HOPE OF FULNESS OF LIFE

SILENCE

THANKSGIVING

XVI God's Holy Spirit is adequate

It is useful to go back again and again to the teaching in the first chapter about the method of relaxation because unless you are really relaxed the mind will wander. I think that in the process of learning to be relaxed there comes a stage when there seems to be a build up of tension. If in the middle of a meditation you find yourself becoming aware of a sense of strain don't force yourself to go on. Move in your chair and get comfortable, take one or two deep breaths, relax and start again. It is very important to learn to relax again, to let all strain go. If you can learn to do this and to start again really relaxed in mind it is a step forward.

WE WAIT ON THEE, HOLY SPIRIT WITHIN

SILENCE

THANKSGIVING

The promises given to us about the Holy Spirit were very definite. The Holy Spirit is the spirit of God, His own spirit. Our Lord speaks of sending the Holy Spirit to us and St. Paul again and again speaks of the presence of God's Holy Spirit in all the world.

The spirit of God is all pervading; it is not only with us if we believe, but is in everyone, in every single soul in the world.

We often speak of the power of the Holy Spirit, but a better word than power would be "adequacy". The Holy Spirit which is within us and in all the world is always adequate to any of our needs. It is the Holy Spirit Himself who gives the power. It is His life, His joy, His goodness, His beauty, His wisdom, which is the power.

TEACH US TO KNOW THE ADEQUACY OF THY HOLY SPIRIT WITHIN

SILENCE

THANKSGIVING

I do not think there are any limits to the power of the Holy Spirit in our lives. There is in every one of us, in our human nature, a power which is terrific, a greatness that we have not grasped yet. We so seldom see real greatness coming out in people, that when we do we are full of enthusiasm. Everybody talks about St. Francis, they enthuse about him and his holiness and his remarkable character, and yet that greatness is possible for every human being because we have the power of God within us. We ought to expect it much more often than we do.

When we worry, we are behaving as though God was not real and when we get angry or when we have hatred in our hearts, it means we have forgotten that the power of God's Holy Spirit is within us. We have to learn to be so certain of God that we can turn to Him and think of Him and the power of His life within us instead of having these negative thoughts and spoiling our own lives and those of other people.

St. John of the Cross says "Where there is no love, put love". But how are we to put love there? By meditating on love, then this love will grow in our minds and hearts and will have its influence on other people. Where there is no glory in a home we can put glory by allowing glory to come deep into our own hearts through meditation. We can learn, by turning again and again to the inner sanctuary, to know the power of the Holy Spirit within.

It is enormously helpful to let your heart sing for joy at the thought of God's life being at work within. Even if we have not got to that stage it is a good thing to meditate on the beauty and love and joy of God's spirit until it becomes something real within. When we learn to put our faith in Him it comes out into expression in greater joy.

It is a very good thing to try to train yourself to allow the first consciousness of a new day to be the thought of the presence of God's spirit within you and to let your heart go out to Him in praise and thanksgiving. You can, for instance, say the word "Joy" over and over, and words like "I will rejoice that Thou art ever at work within me" can always be added to the meditation you are using.

As you go forth from a meditation of this kind and face the world around you, you face it with a consciousness at the back of your mind of an adequacy and power to do well what you have to do during the day. God is everywhere, interested in everything we do and His strength and His wisdom and His capability are there within us.

IN THY PRESENCE IS FULNESS OF JOY

SILENCE

THANKSGIVING

XVII   *The way thoughts influence us*

We need to realise that we all have something to give towards the spirit of our community and that we all receive something; we both give and receive. This spirit which helps people, this community spirit, is something very real. Just as a child in a family is affected if there is quarrelling going on—his mind is affected by the atmosphere even though he may have heard nothing of the actual quarrel—so in a community our thoughts affect one another. So we meditate on the things that are good, things that are happy, things that are of God.

INFINITE SPIRIT OF LOVE, I WOULD KNOW THEE WITHIN

SILENCE

THANKSGIVING

We can vary this meditation using words like "Infinite spirit of joy" or of peace, capability or wisdom—whatever you want to come out into expression. Meditation is not something pious; if we persevere we shall find that it affects everything we do, in a very practical way.

You can try this out in your daily life. Put it to the test and you will find that it is real. If you have to go for an interview or to give a talk just be still and take a meditation like this. You will find that it will surprise you. You will find yourself calm as you never thought you could be.

It is amazing that in spite of all the teaching about psychology and about the human mind so little has been done on teaching people how to use their minds intelligently, not only to help themselves but also to help other people.

In Japan the monks go into the schools and teach the children to think positively about their lessons, and the result is that the children look forward to learning because they see it is going to be of value to them in life. We have nothing like that in this country, in fact we very often tell children that they are slow and we put thoughts of weakness and feebleness into their minds. In that way we hinder their development.

We know that suggestion goes very deep and we also know that it can have a very drastic effect. If a Witch Doctor tells a primitive African that he is going to die that evening, he just lies down and dies. The suggestion is strong enough for that to happen. And we do just the same. When doctors have no remedy to offer someone who is ill, say with cancer, they just say: "This is uncurable, he will die in a few months", and this suggestion goes very deep. Whether or not the patient is told about it, he is surrounded with the thought that he will die, and so he does.

So when someone is ill, or when we ourselves are ill, it is tremendously important to think positively. We must have real expectation when we meditate, that something is going to come out of it, a hope that is joyful and strong.

I WAIT IN GREAT EXPECTATION HOLY SPIRIT WITHIN

SILENCE

THANKSGIVING

I believe that it is very important for us to understand the power of negative thoughts to hinder people from getting better. Someone who had been coming to one of my meditation groups for some time and who I thought had got hold of meditation was very badly affected by her doctor's negative attitude. She had a slight heart attack and her doctor thoroughly frightened her by telling her that she must be very careful not to put herself under any strain; she must not bend down, must not lift, must not do this and must not do that. The result was that she lived in constant fear of another heart attack.

It is no use living with a fear like that, you have got to get rid of it. The only way to do this is by realising that God's healing life is at work within and that His life is completely adequate to the situation. That is one of the things that meditation teaches us, to see the full picture, not only of the evil but of the power which works within to triumph over all evil.

I remember when I was a boy going out into a field of wheat which had been planted a long time. It had hardly begun to grow because there had been a drought, but the previous night there had been a deluge and as I stood in that field I could sense a feeling of movement. There was life moving in all those blades of wheat just showing above the soil. I have often thought if I could have had a tape recorder there with me sensitive enough to hear the movement of life I could have amplified it and brought it to the hearing of people. That is going on all the time, life in us and in everything, and always working to express more and more life. If we think of God's life in that way then we shall overcome all our negative thinking.

INFINITE LIFE WITHIN, I TRUST IN THEE

SILENCE

THANKSGIVING

XVIII *Adoration and Worth-ship*

WE WORSHIP AND ADORE THEE, O GOD

SILENCE

THANKSGIVING

I have emphasised the importance of starting the day by letting your heart go out to God in praise and thanksgiving. Our prayers would be of a much higher quality if we could grasp the fact that prayer is an attitude of adoration. "Our Father, hallowed be Thy name" is really an attitude of adoration. It is not a request that God should do anything, it is our attitude to God, which of course is part of worship.

The more we think of Him, His goodness, His longing for justice and righteousness and of the calmness and joy of His spirit, the more we are drawn to adore Him and to let our hearts go out to Him in thankfulness and praise. The prayer which we are led to in meditation is very often spoken of as affective prayer, the theological term for the prayer of affection, our affection towards God. As we persevere in meditation, and God becomes more real, I think there are times when we want just to be still in an attitude of adoration, an attitude of affection towards God.

So let us be still and hold in our minds just these words—

HOLY SPIRIT WITHIN

SILENCE

THANKSGIVING

Our church services would be much more meaningful if we realised the true purpose of worship. Worship is the adoration that we give to God, our hymns of praise, psalms and the attitude that we have to God, but it is something else as well. Worship is also offering to God something that is worthy of him (worth-ship), something that expresses His purpose for the world. This is a real side of worship that we don't think about nearly enough.

Meditation helps us to enter into this spirit of worship. We believe that the Holy Spirit is within: intellectually we know this, but it is extraordinary how most of us fail to let it be something real in our life. The Holy Spirit dwells within us, not like a bird in a cage making its home within; it is in us in order to express itself. Until it is given a chance to come out into expression nothing happens at all, we remain, as it were, part of a dead creation.

We must sow if we are to reap. Everything that happens has a cause. Nothing comes out of nothing. People plead for peace in the world but they do not realise that the seeds of peace have to be sown. The seeds of peace are justice and love. If only people would begin to think, for thinking must come before anything can be done. If the power of the Holy Spirit is to come into expression in our lives we must sow seeds of love, joy, peace, beauty, wisdom and so on by choosing to think about these qualities of the Holy Spirit.

Whenever you find anyone with a deeply developed spiritual life, you will find that in his life he is expressing only what has gone into him. You can never give until you have learned to receive, and you cannot give any more than you have received. In our prayer life and in our thought life we are opening ourselves to receive what God is always waiting to give us.

WE THANK THEE THAT THY LIFE IS NOW GROWING WITHIN US

SILENCE

THANKSGIVING

XIX Overcoming negative thoughts with joy

In meditation we aim at being receptive, open to receive the truth about God's Holy Spirit within. This receptive silence is not just inactivity of mind, as when we are trying to go to sleep, it is a silence of expectation. We need to expect that we shall enter into a deeper knowledge of God and of His life always within us and around us.

As you continue to practise meditation, I think you will find that it becomes easier to relax both your body and your mind. As you relax the body you find yourself breathing a little more slowly and somehow you let go all thinking and allow the mind to be just in an expectant mood.

HELP ME TO BE MORE ALIVE TO THY LIFE

SILENCE

THANKSGIVING

Although we should know that God's spirit is always at work and is always adequate to our needs, we find it very difficult to overcome negative thoughts. We are all of us liable to form habits of thought and these habits sink very deeply into the mind. If something frightening happens to us we probably feel it is inevitable that we shall feel frightened. Or if somebody is very unkind and difficult we can easily regard it as normal to feel resentment. Since we tend to accept feelings such as these as normal we usually make very little effort to change them. We are seldom aware how deeply emotions such as antagonism or suspicion go down into the subconscious mind, but these negative feelings are very harmful to our character and as well as affecting our character they very often affect our bodies. It is these habits of thought which are responsible for a large amount of disease.

Because it is difficult to overcome these negative feelings we rather take it for granted that nothing can be done about them. But we should never do this. God's creative spirit is at work and part of its work is to build up our characters until we reflect His character, His love, His calmness, His forgivingness, the very opposite of those negative feelings. Through the work of God's Holy Spirit we can be made whole.

LET THY CREATIVE SPIRIT WORK IN US TO MAKE US WHOLE

SILENCE

THANKSGIVING

I do not want you to think of these deep emotional states with any sense of blame. I think we must just realise that they are things which spoil our character, and I cannot help thinking that every one of us has had them. But they can be overcome.

If we think of those people who attain to anything of the perfection that God purposes for us, we realise how marvellous human beings can be. So we ought to have very high ideals for ourselves. We too can enter into the joy which comes when our relationships with other people are happier. Joy and happiness ought to be the mark of a Christian.

CLEANSE THE THOUGHTS OF OUR HEARTS THAT WE MAY KNOW THY JOY WITHIN

SILENCE

THANKSGIVING

XX Righteousness

TEACH US TO KNOW THY RIGHTEOUSNESS, DEAR LORD

SILENCE

THANKSGIVING

A short time ago I was given a little book containing a series of broadcast talks given by Martin Luther King over the Canadian broadcasting system. There is a foreword to the book by his widow, which she ends with the words: "He tried to be a Drum Major for justice, a Drum Major for peace, a Drum Major for righteousness. Remember him as a man who refused to lose faith in the ultimate redemption of mankind". That is a marvellous epitaph to a very great person. No one could ever want anything greater.

This word "righteousness", meaning justice and love, comes again and again all through the Bible, the Old Testament and the New. It comes again and again in the psalms.

"They shall come and shall declare His righteousness" (Psalm 22. 31).

"He will never suffer the righteous to be moved" (Psalm 55. 22).

"Lead me, Lord, in Thy righteousness" (Psalm 5. 8).

"Hear me when I call, oh God of my righteousness" (Psalm 4. 1).

"Thou, Lord, wilt bless the righteous" (Psalm 5. 12).

"The righteous God trieth the hearts and reins" (Psalm 7, 9).

"He shall judge the world in righteousness" (Psalm 9. 8).

God is righteousness. "The Lord our righteousness" (Jeremiah 23. 6). Righteousness is justice and love, the spirit of all goodness. Where there is righteousness between people there is goodness and care and concern for others and peace and sharing of things. If we really love a person and have any sense of justice we cannot sit down and enjoy a good meal if the person we love has nothing to eat. If every one of us in the world were alive to the spirit of righteousness within us it would mean that no one would be allowed to starve, it would mean the end of wars and cruelty of every kind. That spirit of righteousness—right relationships between people—would bring God's Kingdom on earth and all the horrors of the world today would come to an end.

Every human being comes into the world with the spirit of God within him, and the potentiality to grow into the likeness of God. But that potentiality needs to be developed if it is to be brought out into expression. The tragedy about a country like China is that every one of those millions of people could be growing into the likeness of God, but they are waiting for the understanding and the knowledge which will enable the spirit of God within to come out into expression.

I believe that we need to think and to use our imagination to get a vision of God's spirit alive and at work throughout the whole human race. After all, this was what the prophets of the Old Testament were trying to do when they spoke about the purpose of God and of the Kingdom of God. They all believed that God's purpose for the world was perfection and wholeness, in which His life and His righteousness were to be expressed in the life of the human race. Abraham was promised that and began to think about it and to prepare his family for it. It was also the great hope of the Jews that one day all the nations of the earth would be blessed. "I shall be satisfied when I awake, with Thy likeness" (Psalm 17. 15).

OPEN OUR EYES, DEAR LORD, TO THY PURPOSE
IN ALL THE WORLD

SILENCE

THANKSGIVING

There is a word that has been bandied about very freely and people have been thinking a great deal about it—and that is "participation". Nearly all the students who are demonstrating are doing it because they want participation in the plans that are being made for them, they want to share in arranging things in schools and universities. This is a very important thing; it expresses the dissatisfaction the young people today are feeling. The last few years have been years of demonstration, student rebellions and demands for participation. After all, the future is much nearer to the young than it is to us. It is they who are going to take part in it. How few people realise how much good there is in all this.

Everybody with knowledge, experience and wisdom has something to contribute, whatever their age. But instead of responding to God's spirit we so often fail to help Him overcome the evils of the world. Instead of carrying out His purpose we allow ourselves to be turned aside from it. We do not persevere because we think the task is too hard for us, or maybe we fail to understand what we ought to be working for. But His life is filling all life, His life within every human being in all the world is a continuing purpose always working towards the perfect and full expression of His life. If we were able to achieve that, the world would become what He intends it to become—perfect and whole.

LEAD ME, OH LORD, IN THY RIGHTEOUSNESS

SILENCE

THANKSGIVING

XXI *Praying for people who are ill*

MY LIFE IS TRIUMPHANT LIFE AT WORK
WITHIN YOU

SILENCE

THANKSGIVING

When we pray for those who are ill, however serious the illness may be, we should always remember that the medical point of view is only one part of the picture. The doctors may say: "There is no hope, this is incurable" and the disease may be incurable according to medical science, but nothing is impossible to God. I know this because three times in my life I have had conditions which the doctors said were incurable.

It is vitally important to have this positive attitude towards illness because the power of suggestion is so great. We cannot keep our thoughts to ourselves, and just as a sinking feeling of hopelessness will convey itself to the person who is ill, so too will our feeling of confidence. If our attitude is that God's healing life is in the person and is entirely adequate to all their needs, they will sense our feeling of confidence. If we can convey that thought to their mind we shall help them enormously.

When we pray for those who are ill we do not say "They are going to be healed". But how can we help them? We do not do what the Christian Scientists do, which is to say that the evil is not real. We do not attempt to deny that they are ill, but we are at the same time, very much aware of God's life within them always working to overcome sickness and disease, as it is working to overcome every evil. His purpose is that all those evil things should be overcome.

So, when praying for someone who is ill, troubled, or afraid, do not resist the illness or the fear or whatever it may

67

be. Just be aware that God's infinite love within them is adequate to all their needs, whatever they may be.

It is very easy to be possessive when we pray for someone we love, but I believe that the answer to our prayer comes just at the moment when we give that person over entirely to God. A possessive love does not trust God and so often when we pray for things in our life we are possessive, we are not at all prepared to trust God. Possessive love is really destructive.

So let us in our meditation centre our thoughts on God's infinite love and adequacy.

I WOULD TRUST IN THE COMPLETE ADEQUACY OF THY LIFE WITHIN TO SUPPLY ALL MY NEEDS

SILENCE

THANKSGIVING

If we ourselves are ill it is of course just as important to think positively. Before we begin to meditate we should always be sure to get out of our minds any thoughts of anything imperfect or ugly or unpleasant. Therefore if we are ill we do not want to think of the illness, we try to put that as far as we can out of our minds. We do not ask that God will take away our pain because that is impressing upon the mind that we have pain. Instead we try to impress upon the deep mind the feeling of God's activity in healing and wholeness and vitality and life. When we meditate in this way the result is that it gives us a calmness and freedom from fear and a positive attitude of mind, and all of this works for our healing.

I would like to share with you part of a letter I received from a woman I have known since her childhood. She has done brilliantly in her work which has taken her all over the world, although she has had to contend with precarious health for years. Recently she had to go into hospital for a very serious operation and for a time her life was in danger. She now writes to thank me for my prayers and the help that I have given her over the years. She says "In hospital I began to have some real understanding of what you meant when you talked about the power of the Holy Spirit within. Right from the start and during the whole time I was in hospital I had an absolutely overwhelming conviction and certainty that everything would be all right. It was not a specific conviction that the operation would be a success but that everything would happen for the best for me. And almost more remarkable that I knew I would be given the strength to face whatever was necessary". This indeed proved to be the case; in fact her recovery after the operation was so successful that the surgeons were quite excited about it.

If a person really perseveres in meditation as she had done for a good many years, it gives a feeling of confidence of God's life being at work and a tremendous sense of positive faith.

I GIVE THEE REST, I SET THEE FREE, I MAKE THEE WHOLE

SILENCE

THANKSGIVING

XXII Helping people who are ill

THY HEALING LIFE WITHIN ME IS
ALWAYS AT WORK

SILENCE

THANKSGIVING

There are so many people—we come across them all the time—who have no idea of how their attitude of mind affects their health. They perhaps have no faith in the power of God to heal, in fact no idea of how thinking affects the body.

How are we to help people like that? When we go to see them we shall probably find that they begin by talking about themselves and are entirely negative in the way in which they speak about their illness. As a rule it is better at first to say very little, to listen and to let them pour out their hearts and all the trouble that is in them. That itself can be an enormous relief, just to talk to someone who is really prepared to listen.

But we want to go on to something more positive than that, so before seeing them again we need to spend time during our times of meditation, holding that person in the silence before God. We do not ask God to do this or that for them, we just try to think of them becoming more conscious of the adequacy of His power and life at work within them. Then our next visit to them will be different. We shall go intending that they shall not pour out again all their troubles and all the details of their illness; but instead we shall begin by trying to get a positive attitude.

We encourage them to think positively of their own symptoms and situation, to realise that there is not only the illness or the pain but that besides this there is the life of God's Holy Spirit within them which is always working for their healing. The picture of them with the details of the disease is only part of the picture. When we bring God in and His healing work then we have a picture of the whole of the situation. So do not let a person go on and on talking about themselves and their illness but challenge them to think of God and the power of His life and His purpose to heal. It is a continuing work that He is doing within, always healing, always loving, always with the hope that we shall become the perfect expression of His own life. We ourselves try to let these thoughts sink deeply into our own mind and because mind touches mind our thoughts will help the person we are concerned about.

BE STILL AND KNOW MY LIFE AT WORK WITHIN

SILENCE

THANKSGIVING

A few days ago I was talking to someone who has started many very active meditation groups in her area. She was telling me that she and several others who are able to give the time, meet in one another's houses to meditate together whenever someone known to a group member is ill. If someone is to have an operation then they will meet every morning for a few days before the operation and on the day of the operation, spending perhaps a quarter of an hour praying for them, having let the person know they will be doing this. Nothing can be a greater help to someone undergoing an operation than to know that a faithful band will be meeting to uphold them and strengthen them.

Prayer of this kind helps people to get the best from what the doctors are doing for them. When members of a group are ill and experience this concern for their wellbeing it leads to a deeper fellowship amongst the group. They always remember the way in which they were helped and that strengthens the band of Christians.

THINE INFINITE SPIRIT IS NOW WITHIN ME

SILENCE

THANKSGIVING

XXIII   *Being truly human*

I WOULD BE MORE AWARE OF THY TRIUMPHANT POWER AT WORK WITHIN ME

The test of the reality of our religion is not how many times we go to church nor even how many prayers we say, but how far we are growing into God's likeness.   That means not that we are looking for something for our own aggrandisement, but are looking to God, wanting to become the kind of people He wants us to be.

But how can we possibly ever be like that?   How can we possibly begin to grow into God's likeness?   We ought to think a great deal about this.   The trouble is that we all have our own ideas of God.   Very often our ideas are not big enough nor simple enough.   We cannot help thinking of Him as far away and we think of words like "Godliness" and "The glory of God" as something quite beyond us.

In our services we sing "Glory to the Father, Son and Holy Ghost" and most people think of this as the glorification of God.   When they hear words like "The earth shall be filled with the glory of God" they picture His glory shining out in brilliancy and light.   But this is a completely wrong idea; there is no reference to any sort of light.   The glory of God is His goodness; and not only His goodness but His love, His wisdom, His calmness and peace . . . we can go on with any number of words.   But what I want you to realise, to think about very carefully, is that these words are ones which we apply to human beings.   When God wanted to show Himself to men the only way he could do it was by sending Jesus Christ, a perfect human being, to live in the world amongst us, and in Jesus Christ we see God.   "He that hath seen me hath seen the Father".   So the more our spiritual life grows and develops, the less pious we become, and the more truly human.

St. Paul speaks of his deep longing "that if possible we may bring every man up to his full maturity in Christ Jesus". If we do grow into the full maturity of which we are capable we shall then become like Christ, not in any pious way, but just completely and fully human, for in Christ is revealed to us the full possibility of our human nature.

We shall now have as a meditation, or a prayer

THAT IN CHRIST WE MAY SEE WHAT IT IS TO BE TRULY HUMAN

SILENCE

THANKSGIVING

I want us to think a bit more about this word "human". If we hear about a person who does something horrible we say "How beastly!" showing that we realise that something horrible is not human but beastly (hard luck on the animals). Words like inhuman, degrading, and unnatural show that we understand human nature to be incapable of being like this, of being really cruel and unkind.

It is our job as Christians to help people to become fully human, because only by becoming thoroughly human can we become like God, because God has the characteristics of perfect humanity. To be truly human is to express the glory of God revealed to us by Jesus Christ in His life.

This is why we meditate on the glory of God and its expression in Christ, "Christ within, our hope of glory". We meditate in this way not merely to help us to change our own characters but because of other people whom we meet and who catch things from our minds. Let us take the meditation—

THOU ART EVER AT WORK BRINGING FORTH THY LIKENESS WITHIN ME

SILENCE

THANKSGIVING

XXIV *Bringing in the Kingdom of heaven*

OPEN OUR EYES DEAR LORD TO THE GLORY OF THY PURPOSE FOR US

In these chapters we have been learning that if we use our minds in a particular way to impress certain thoughts upon our subconscious minds these thoughts will come out into expression in our lives. If we impress thoughts of peace, joy, capability, calmness and so on, upon our subconscious mind, we shall express these qualities in our lives.

If we think about it, this concentration on ourselves, on how we think and feel, is a selfish occupation, a selfish purpose. Yet if our purpose is to become the kind of people God wants us to become, then it is quite all right for us to centre our thoughts on ourselves in this way, learning to bring God's life out into expression.

But we must not remain self-centred because religion is not just for ourselves, it is not just a question of being concerned about our own souls; we must look outwards, we must be concerned about the whole human family. God's purpose is for the whole world. It is very important that we should have high ideals for the world. I think this is one of the most important things we can possibly think about.

I have been reading a book by Stephen Neill, and he says that the best way of thinking of the spirit of God within the whole creation is to think of Him as energy. It is the energy of God which brought creation into being and is behind and underneath it, substanding the whole creation all the time. The spirit of God fills the universe and there is nowhere where God is not, where His energy is not at work.

I think this was what Our Lord meant when He said "Ye shall receive power when the Holy Spirit has come upon you".

TEACH US TO LIVE BY THE POWER OF THY HOLY SPIRIT WITHIN

SILENCE

THANKSGIVING

If what Jesus said is true, why are we such poor creatures? Because we are you know. It is a most extraordinary thing that as Christians we have not got a greater sense of power. Yet how often we are completely faithless. Again and again we are quite hopeless about the world. How often Christian people say "Oh the world is a dreadful place, it is terrible, horrible." But we are content to let things go on the way they are although we realise that the world is not anything like the kind of world God wants it to be. We just sit back and make the best of it, and worry very little about the rest of the people in the world.

It is so easy to let ourselves become involved in the evil of the world, to be a part of it. So often we are completely unconscious of the things that are wrong with the world. For instance when we go shopping, say for oranges, how many of us are concerned where they came from? We see a kind that is particularly luscious and lovely so we buy it, without thinking about the people who grew those oranges and packed them and looked after them all the time they were growing on trees out in South Africa, where there is apartheid and the coloured labourers are paid wretchedly low wages and are not treated as human beings at all. By buying these oranges we have become involved in the totally unchristian attitude between men who have white skins and men who have coloured skins. Or if we go and buy eggs, how often do we think of the battery hens never given a chance to run about, hardly allowed to move, just half a square foot of room in the battery for each one? They have to live like that until they are taken away and killed, then there is all the cruelty of the killing. There is a law which requires poultry to be stunned before being killed, but the law is not always put in effect. How often when we buy meat do we think about the terrible cruelty these animals have suffered?

Surely this is where, if we were more aware of the Holy Spirit, He would make us sensitive to what is within the world, and we should either make a protest or see that we are not involved with the evil. He would enable us to do everything as Christians, in fact to be responsible people as members of His Church. If we are to live as Christians we need to think of the life of God at work in the whole world, working to overcome what is evil.

It is His purpose to perfect the world, and there are signs in the whole creation that there is gradual progress towards perfection.

Our Lord said, "I am the Way, walk ye in it". He wants us to be fellow workers with Him, working to bring in the Kingdom of Heaven on earth.

Let us take for our last meditation our Lord's words.

I AM THE WAY, WALK YE IN IT

SILENCE

THANKSGIVING

Praise God in His holiness, praise Him in all the world. We praise and worship Thee, dear Lord, and give Thee thanks for all our fellowship.

Let us go forth in peace.